Starting Agile

Finding Your Path

Mark Shead

Starting Agile
Finding Your Path

Mark Shead

ISBN 978-1-945121-09-8

Contents

CONTENTS

Introduction

I help organizations write software more efficiently. This usually involves improving agility. Teams that I coach are often full of people who have learned Agile through training in a particular set of practices or by watching what other Agile teams do. This leads to a common problem. Everyone knows **what** they should do without really understanding **why** they are doing it. This may work fine for a time, but you aren't Agile unless you can quickly adapt to new situations. The **what** is going to continually change. Without fully understanding the **why**, it is difficult to retain agility and adapt.

> *A young couple was hosting Thanksgiving. The wife asked her husband to cut off both ends of the ham and put them in the pan along the side before cooking it. He asked why, and she admitted that she wasn't sure. It was just the way her family cooked a ham. When her mother arrived, they asked her. She wasn't sure either. She had learned the practice from her mother. When the grandmother walked in, they asked her. "Well, back then my pan wasn't quite long enough for the ham," she said, "but it fit perfectly if we just cut a few inches off each end."*

1

Two generations needlessly cut off the ends of the ham, but it did no harm. It was just an extra action, a short ceremony that no longer served any purpose other than preserving a childhood memory. However, I frequently find "Agile" teams with entrenched rituals, rules, routines, red-tape, and regulations that are incredibly harmful and no one questions why they are there. It is not uncommon to find groups doing the exact opposite of what Agile principles suggest. Often, a team starts with a practice that supports agility in their particular situation. Perhaps an Agile coach suggests a practice without fully explaining why, maybe it is selected by a previous team focused on Agile principles and values, or maybe it is just luck. As time passes the situation changes and the practice is modified without a good understanding of the why behind the original practice. The team eventually ends up with ways of working that are based on a previous practice instead of the principles which justified the original. There is a game called "Telephone" where a message is whispered from person to person that drifts further and further from the original meaning with each repetition. If you don't continuously reconcile your practices against your principles, your organization is essentially playing this slow game of telephone.

I wrote this book to give teams a foundation for starting with Agile by focusing on the **why**. Books that are all **why** and no **what** are not very interesting to read because most of us are looking for practical application. A book without any **what** is not particularly engaging.

With that in mind, this book is going to start by answering the question, "What is Agile?" That is the primary goal of the next chapter. With that foundation in place, the rest of this book is going to look at some common practices teams find useful in following Agile. We are going to look at general practices (the **what**) that many teams find useful while making sure that we focus on the **why** behind each practice. Keep in mind that the practices themselves should be flexible. They are only a means to follow Agile values and principles.

What is Agile?

Many things get called Agile–especially by people who are selling something. If you ask the makers of paper products, they will tell you that to be Agile you need to write user stories on the sticky note cards (that they just happen to sell). If you ask a consultant, you will likely hear that it is a methodology for developing software that your organization can learn (if you buy their services). And if, for some strange reason, you decide to ask the makers of orthopedic shoes to define Agile, you will likely learn that the key to being Agile is meetings where everyone stands up. Obviously, the more comfortable your shoes, the more Agile your team.

You can find the actual definition of Agile in the Agile Manifesto at agilemanifesto.org. The Manifesto makes it clear that Agile is not a methodology. It is not a specific way of doing software development. It is not a framework or a process. In fact, most of the things marketed as Agile tend to miss the point of what Agile actually is.

Agile is a set of values and principles.

The discussion around Agile often revolves around following different practices, using various methodologies, and even developing with specific tools. While these things might help a team that is trying to follow Agile, they are not Agile in and of themselves. For example, while a team may find that having a daily standup is helpful, the standup is only "Agile" to the extent that it is the result of a team following the Agile principles and values.

Once you understand this, it is easy to see that Agile is really a collection of beliefs that teams can use for making decisions about how to do the work of developing software. While this means the term Agile gets subjected to a great deal of abuse when people claim that this or that is **the** way to be Agile, it also means that, if you truly understand what Agile is, it is surprisingly flexible. Agile does not make decisions for you. Instead, it gives a foundation for teams to make their own decisions in ways that improve the process of developing software.

The Agile Manifesto is only 68 words and simply says that we can develop software better by valuing the items on the left side of the list more than the items on the right side. This is what the Agile Manifesto says:

> We are uncovering better ways of developing software by doing it and helping others do it. Through this work we have come to value:

- Individuals and interactions over processes and tools
- Working software over comprehensive documentation
- Customer collaboration over contract negotiation

- Responding to change over following a plan

    That is, while there is value in the items on the right, we value the items on the left more.

In addition to the values of the Manifesto, there are 12 principles that support the values. Remember, the principles are very general and are less focused on telling you what to do than they are on guiding you to a good decision in your particular situation.

The principles are:

- Our highest priority is to satisfy the customer through early and continuous delivery of valuable software.
- Welcome changing requirements, even late in development. Agile processes harness change for the customer's competitive advantage.
- Deliver working software frequently, from a couple of weeks to a couple of months, with a preference to the shorter timescale.
- Business people and developers must work together daily throughout the project.
- Build projects around motivated individuals. Give them the environment and support they need, and trust them to get the job done.
- The most efficient and effective method of conveying information to and within a development team is face-to-face conversation.

- Working software is the primary measure of progress.
- Agile processes promote sustainable development. The sponsors, developers, and users should be able to maintain a constant pace indefinitely.
- Continuous attention to technical excellence and good design enhances agility.
- Simplicity–the art of maximizing the amount of work not done–is essential.
- The best architectures, requirements, and designs emerge from self-organizing teams.
- At regular intervals, the team reflects on how to become more effective, then tunes and adjusts its behavior accordingly.

Agile Decisions

Since Agile is a collection of values and principles, its real utility is in giving people a common foundation for making decisions about the best way to develop software. For example, consider a new project that is in discussions about how to get the requirements from the business owner. The suggested approach is to require the business owner write down all the requirements and sign off on them before beginning the work. A team that is following Agile would say:

While that might work, is that consistent with our belief that we should value customer collaboration over contract negotiation? And doesn't it violate our principle that says the developers should be working with the business owners every day? How can we make this decision in a way that is consistent with our values and the principles we follow?

Now let us consider a developer who is working on implementing a feature for the business owner. The developer realizes they need a database to make the feature work. The first idea that comes to mind is to stop work on the feature and build out a robust database layer that will handle not only the needs of the feature but also provide lots of support for other development that will be needed to build later features. If the developer believes in the Agile values and is trying to follow Agile principles, they would think:

 But building out this layer means I will have to delay delivering what the customer can see as valuable software that implements this particular feature. If I can find a way to build just what is necessary to deliver this feature, it will better align with my principles.

When you have a team that is following Agile they will be making hundreds of decisions each week in the way described above. That is what it means to be Agile–making each decision based on the principles and values that the team has decided to follow.

How you make decisions matters. You cannot try to short-circuit things by taking decisions made by another team, blindly doing what they decided to do, and hope to get the same results. When a team makes decisions based on the Agile principles and values, they should end up with a particular way of doing their work that is based on their unique situation. Simply trying to mimic another team's actions and practices won't make your team Agile.

After World War II, Melanesian islanders were observed trying to bring cargo planes and their supplies from the sky by mimicking the practices they had seen performed during the war. This included clearing the forest to make a landing strip complete with full-size planes made out of straw. They also created structures that mimicked a control tower out of bamboo and had someone sit in it wearing headphones fashioned from coconuts.

Teams can easily fall into a similar type of "cargo cult" mentality when it comes to Agile. The things that are easy to notice in a highly functional Agile team are the practices they are using, but the practices a team uses are only the *result* of following Agile principles and values. The specific practices a team happens to be using are far less important than the reasons or foundation behind those practices. As time goes by, a good Agile team is probably going to change and refine the practices they use.

A team might start with SCRUM and later determine that Kanban is a better fit for delivering value to their customers. A team might begin standing up in a daily meeting and later decide it works better for everyone to stay sitting down. Another team might start out using Planning Poker to estimate story size and later do away with story points and simply split stories to be approximately the same size.

It is not useless to look at practices being used by teams that are performing well, but you cannot go looking for practices to make you Agile. Your principles and values are what will make you Agile. You have to look for practices that support your principles and values. The method used to select your practices is what determines whether you are being Agile or not. If a practice is being selected because it looks like a good way to follow Agile principles, it is probably a good place to start. The same practice can work poorly for a team if it is selected for the wrong reason.

So what is Agile?

Agile is a set of values and principles.

How does a team become Agile?

They make their decisions based on Agile values and principles.

The decision-making process is how a team becomes Agile. The values and principles have enough flexibility to allow teams in a wide variety of organizations to develop software in the ways that work best for their particular situation while also providing enough direction to help each team progress toward their full potential.

Becoming More Agile

So how do you "make your team Agile?" Well, you don't. At least you don't just tell everyone to be Agile, make a cake, print t-shirts, give everyone a certificate, declare success, and move on. Agile is not some type of award that teams win after jumping through certain hoops. The whole point is to develop the capability to respond efficiently to change. This is not something that you can just do and then move on. Obtaining agility requires an ongoing effort to maintain the capability of handling the unknown future. What you should be striving for is is an environment and culture that is always taking gradual but steady steps toward increased agility. If every day you increase your ability to respond to future change, then you are making progress with Agile.

With that in mind, we can slightly refine our question to: How do you become more Agile? There are two primary ways to increase your agility. The first way to become more Agile is to set your teams up so they have the opportunity and motivation to continually improve. Teams need the ability to make small experiments and access to the information necessary to judge the success or failure of those experiments. They need to have (or be given the freedom to create) tools and processes that make it easy to get the feedback they need. This is not necessarily as complicated as it sounds. There are many ways to get feedback, and it can be as simple as, *"if we record when we start on a task, we can figure out when something is taking longer than normal and may need more of our attention."*

The second way to become more Agile is to implement practices that will help your team follow Agile principles. For example, since we have a principle that says face-to-face is the most effective way for teams to communicate, maybe a team room would be a good practice to follow. Since we have a principle that teams should reflect on the past and adjust for the future, maybe the practice of retrospectives is a good way to follow that principle.

In the rest of this book, we are going to look at a number of practices that teams find helpful in the continual process of becoming more Agile week after week. Even more important than the practice, we will also look at the Agile Principles that have led teams to those practices. The reason this is so important is that the value you get out of a particular practice is dependent on why you are implementing the practice. If you implement a practice in order to follow a particular set of Agile principles, it leaves you in a good position to grow, adapt, and continue to improve. If you follow a practice just because you read it in a book, you are not setting your team up for long-term success in dealing with change in the future. Blindly following practices makes you more rigid and less Agile, but following principles enables you to evolve the practices to your changing needs.

Visualize Your Work

- Our highest priority is to satisfy the customer through early and continuous delivery of valuable software.
- Welcome changing requirements, even late in development. Agile processes harness change for the customer's competitive advantage.
- The most efficient and effective method of conveying information to and within a development team is face-to-face conversation.

Attempting to follow any of these principles requires having some way of understanding the state of your software development efforts. You cannot continuously deliver valuable software without having some way of knowing what the status is for various pieces of work. You cannot even tell what work is valuable unless you have some way of communicating that X is more valuable than Y. It is difficult for teams to have any type of meaningful conversation about the work if there is not a clear way to see who is doing what. It is hard to welcome changing requirements if you don't know what is currently being worked on, what has been completed, and what has yet to be done.

There are scores of ways to keep track of what a team is working on. However, if we really want to facilitate face-to-face discussion, it is very beneficial to have something that can be viewed by multiple people at the same time. If our priority is to harness change as a competitive advantage, then we need to make it easy to see how our work may be different today than what we thought it was yesterday. If we want to continually deliver software, we need to have an easy way to know what is in the current version and what is coming up next.

A Simple Board

I am going to describe a simple way to visualize your work in order to support the Agile Principles mentioned above. It is a good place to start, but the goal is to support the Agile Principles. If you find a way to change things so your team can better support those principles, by all means, do so.

Take a section of wall or whiteboard and divide it into four sections. One section will be for things you probably want to do, the next section will be for things you are getting ready to do, the next section will be for things the team is currently doing, and the last section will be for things that are completed. You also need an easy way to add or remove a column if you find a way to improve the way you work, so do not create these sections in stone where they cannot be modified. A whiteboard works well because you can write your headings and just rearrange them later. Painters tape works well on a wall because it is easy to pull down and restructure when the need arises.

Should we use software?

Do not overlook the value of a tactile system that you can touch, point at, and move around. Even if you plan to switch to a virtual board, it can be good to start with a physical board that is easy to manipulate and rearrange.

Title the sections:

- Backlog
- To Do
- In Progress
- Complete

Use sticky notes to write down what you are working on and put them under the appropriate headings. You now have a very easy to update, visual, flexible way of keeping track of what is being worked on.

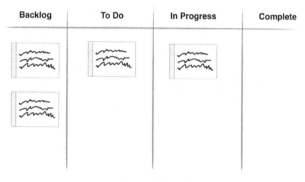

A simple board

Telling Stories

The fact that you are using sticky notes to represent your work places certain constraints on how much information you can record. What should you put on the note? You could try to list the step-by-step details of what you want to do, but that can take a lot of time and space, and you probably will not know what needs to be done until you actually start working on it.

One method that works well for many teams is to think of the note as a very short story that tells how the world will be different from the user perspective when you have successfully completed the work. Here are some example stories:

- A registered user can log in to the application and then change his/her password.
- A user can make a payment using their credit card.
- If the flux capacitor gets locked up, an email is sent to the emergency email address.

An important key for creating stories is to make it easy to tell when it is completed. You do not want to fill the sticky note with all kinds of details that will be worked out in the process of completing the story, but you do want it to be fairly easy to say, "Yes, the application now does this" or "No, we aren't quite finished."

It is vital that stories be written from the user perspective—not the developer. They tell how the user's world will be different when the story is marked complete. Consider the following stories:

- The application has data access objects for the data model.
- A user can register and create an account.
- Spring Security is configured.
- A user with an incorrect password is shown an error message.

It should be easy to spot the stories that are written from the user perspective and see the ones that are written from the developer perspective. The obvious objection is, "But we cannot create an account until we have the data access objects to save the account to the database." This is not quite true. You do not have to build all the data access objects in order to create an account. You only need to build the ones that are necessary to demonstrate the functionality to the user. Why does this matter? Look at the following principles.

- Our highest priority is to satisfy the customer through early and continuous delivery of valuable software.
- Working software is the primary measure of progress.

Working software means it does something for the user. No matter how beautiful our code and architecture, the goal is to create software that gives the user business value. If we use stories that are measuring something that does not result in working software for the user, we are violating our principles. Early delivery of valuable software means we need to focus on the value we can provide today—not on creating infrastructure to provide what we think might be valuable tomorrow. If we prioritize a story to build out a layer of architecture over a story to build something we can deliver to the user, then we are violating our principles.

Creating stories that focus on how the system will be different from the user perspective can be extremely challenging at first—especially when you try to keep the story size small. We will address this in a later chapter, but the takeaway for right now is that your stories need to tell how the user world looks different when the story is done. Doing so follows our principles about being focused on the business value that is being frequently added to the application and helps prevent the creation of code before it is needed.

It can sometimes help to have a template for writing these stories. One popular format is something like the following:

As a _____

I want to _____

So I can _____

Let's see what some of those would look like:

As a registered user
I want to change my password
So I can keep my account secure

As the system
I want to monitor the flux capacitor
So I can notify the emergency address if it locks up

This type of format does a good job of helping you remain focused on how a user wants to be able to interact with your system, so you will often see people referring to stories about their users as "user stories." Notice, there is nothing that keeps you from writing a story about the system itself or other things if the story is still about the user's world. You may find that a different template works better for your team. The goal of using a template is to give some consistency while avoiding any type of writer's block. It is often easier to fill in three blanks than writing the story from scratch.

I would highly recommend at least trying the template

above, but do not stick with it if you find something else that works better for your team. The important thing is to make it easy to know whether you have completed the work or not. A short story about the way the user's world will look and behave when you can mark it as complete is a good way to do that regardless of the particulars that your team decides to use.

> I was once helping a team switch to this style of stories, but one product owner was out the week we started. On his return, he asked one of the developers, "Why does Mark keep sending me this weird poetry?" Evidently he thought I was writing some strange form of Haiku. Forget the Agile coach! Let's get a bard to write some poetry.

Story Points and Story Size

If you follow this approach, you will quickly discover that there can be a lot of variance in how big a story can be. Consider the following two user stories.

As a web visitor
I want to click on the word "Home"
So I can return to the home page

As a web shopper
I want the site to support e-commerce
So I can do everything related to orders

The first story encompasses very little. In fact, the story is so small that it might take about the same amount of time to write the story as it would take to implement it. The second story is huge. It seems to encompass everything from placing orders, handling returns, calculating shipping and taxes, to managing inventory. These examples are obviously two extremes, but they demonstrate that you can write stories that require a small amount of work and you can write stories that require a very large amount of work.

One way to get an idea of how long a story will take is to assign a number of points to the story. Basically, you come up with your best guess. A story that is assigned a 10 will take 10 times as much effort as a story that is assigned a 1. There are lots of ways to come up with these numbers and some teams make something of a game of it. This is not necessarily a bad approach, but it does take time and in most cases, it is not particularly accurate. The value you get out of estimating needs to be compared with how much it costs. I've seen some teams spend up to one-third of their time in a particular week estimating the size of the stories. It is unlikely that these estimates are providing value that exceeds the cost of doing 33% less development.

To minimize the time commitment made to estimating, some teams try to do it really quickly. For example, they might have everyone assigning a number to how big they think a story is and then averaging them with maybe a little discussion on the ones that have a lot of disagreement. Other teams try to size stories with "t-shirt sizes" of Small, Medium, Large, and X-Large.

Aside from the amount of time it takes to estimate, "story points" and "t-shirt sizes" both have an even bigger problem. Trying to estimate the size of stories encourages you to go ahead and leave in big stories that really could be broken down into smaller units of work. Why are big stories a bad thing? If you are following the principle of delivering software on a regular basis, large stories slow this process down. They also make it more difficult to adapt to changing requirements. If you can get a smaller story into production that the customer can start using, they may realize there is a missing requirement or even that they do not want that functionality after all. Small stories let you follow the Agile principles.

Another approach that often works better than story points is to try to make your stories roughly the same size. What that size is depends on your team. You typically don't want your average story size to be more than a few days worth of work. If you see a story that you know is going to take a week or more, it is a strong indicator that it can be split into multiple separate stories.

You may end up with some stories that only take six hours and have an occasional outlier where you run into problems and it ends up taking a week or two. That may seem like quite a range, but once you have some history, you should be able to get an idea of how much time it takes to complete 10 stories if they have all been broken down to what you think will take no more than a few days. The ones that go fast will average out with the ones that take longer.

Small stories also give you faster feedback if it turns out things are much more difficult than they initially look. A particular aspect of functionality may turn out to be much more tricky than it initially looked. You start with a small story that looks like it will take two days, but instead it takes five times as long–ten days. After this discovery, you now have a much better idea of how long it is going to take to do other similar stories. Maybe the business owner will decide there are other parts of the software that are a higher priority. Or maybe, you will decide that you need to take a different approach or use a different type of technology. On the other hand, if you have a large story that you estimate will take ten days and it ends up taking five times as long, you will probably end up doing a lot more work before evaluating your approach and the value of that story. Large stories slow your feedback loop making it harder to adjust to the information you learn in the development process.

Simple Metrics

If you need to capture metrics, the simple board approach works surprisingly well. You can just add the date when you start work on a story to the note. When you finish, add the number of days it took to complete. You will end up with a stack of notes that will give you a pretty good view of how long it takes to complete a story. (You can even arrange them on another wall as a histogram by the number of days they took to complete to give you an idea of what your cycle time bell curve looks like.) This can be useful to give you feedback about how well your team is doing at sizing the stories. It can also be a useful indicator of whether other changes to your processes are helping or hurting your progress.

If over a few months, your stories take an average of three days to complete and you suddenly notice that your average shoots up to eight days, it is worth taking a look at what may have caused that change. Perhaps you have several people out on vacation. Maybe you tried using some new technology, and it is taking a while to handle the learning curve. Maybe you are trying to work on too many things at the same time. Maybe you changed some other aspect of your development process, and it is not working out quite as well as you hoped or causing unexpected side effects. A big change in the average time it takes to complete a story does not directly tell you what is going on, but it can be a useful tool, almost like a speedometer of a car, to identify when changes are helping or hurting the development effort.

Daily Face-to-Face

- The most efficient and effective method of conveying information to and within a development team is face-to-face conversation.
- Business people and developers must work together daily throughout the project.
- Working software is the primary measure of progress.

If your team wants to follow the principles of communicating face-to-face and working together, you are going to have to make sure people actually get together in the same room and talk. Following these principles can become very natural, but many working environments are anything but natural. A great practice to help encourage this is to get everyone together for a brief daily face-to-face meeting with the purpose of making sure that you do not have any communication friction slowing down any of the stories as they move from the to-do to the complete column.

It is not necessary to try to cram in every conversation that needs to occur. The goal is to have a daily meeting that is designed to highlight the conversations and work that are necessary to move each story forward. Most teams refer to this meeting as the daily standup. We are going to also refer to this meeting as the daily face-to-face to help highlight that the principle we are trying to follow is face-to-face communication. There is not any principle that says "teams are more effective when they stand for a meeting." That is not to say that the idea of a standup meeting is not valuable, just that we need to be clear what principles our practices are trying to follow.

Why Stand?

Why do some teams call it a daily standup? As the name implies, a standup meeting is conducted standing up. This is simply an aspect of the practice that many people have found useful because it helps encourage the meetings to be short and to the point. Standing helps make everyone aware if the meeting goes on for too long and also helps to get people up from their desk and away from distractions so everyone can focus on the meeting. Getting your team together even for a short meeting is a pretty big investment. Standing ensures that the meeting will be efficient, focused, and short.

I have participated in meetings where what they call the stand-up is conducted sitting down. The point is not that standing is somehow magic, but if you do a sitting face-to-face meeting you may need to put a little extra effort into making sure everyone is engaged and the conversation stays focused.

A distributed team was doing their daily stand-up on video conference. People tried to stand at their individual desks, but then the cameras only captured their midsection. It didn't take long to decide that sitting face-to-face interactions were far superior to standing stomach-to-stomach meetings.

Calling the meeting a "stand-up" keeps the team focused on the physical position they will assume during the meeting while calling it the "face-to-face" keeps everyone focused on the Agile principles driving the meeting. This is similar to the difference between calling a pool of water a "prone pool" to highlight the position in which most people swim vs. calling it a "swimming pool."

Of course, it is not necessary to go through your organization and force everyone to use the term "daily face-to-face" instead of "daily stand-up." Just be aware that when we use names that obscure the reason behind an activity, we must be extra careful to stay focused on the **why** that is driving that activity.

So, regardless of whether you sit or stand, how long should this daily face-to-face meeting be? For most teams, 15 to 20 minutes seems to be an effective target. Obviously, the length can vary significantly from day to day and from team to team, but trying to hit something near the 15 minute mark is usually reasonable.

One of the reasons you want to keep the daily face-to-face meeting brief is because people need to be fully engaged, and that means they cannot feel as though the meeting is wasting their time. These meetings require a significant commitment for people and if they do not feel they are valuable, you will have a hard time getting people to show up on time.

How to Run a Daily Face-to-Face

Some people like to run face-to-face meetings where every-one tells what they did yesterday and what they are going to do today. This can be helpful because it makes sure that everyone knows what their teammates are working on, but it does have a downside. Think back to how we measure success. If we measure our ability to deliver working code, our face-to-face meetings should have the outcome of helping make the production of that code as efficient as possible. The way we visualize success is by getting stories from the to-do column to the completed column. If that is what we are trying to optimize in the face-to-face meeting, then we need to focus our discussion on the movement of those stories across the board. Meetings that focus on what people are doing are going to carry a lot of overhead that does not contribute to the movement of those stories.

Most companies have cultures and processes that are not designed to make the production of software more efficient. In fact, at many companies you would probably conclude that things have been designed specifically to make the production of software less efficient! When you run a people-centric face-to-face meeting, you often end up investing your time talking about how people are dealing with company culture and processes. The fact that half the team did their mandatory security/sensitivity/assertiveness/humility/acronym or whatever training yesterday and half are going to do it today may need to be mentioned, but only within the context of how it relates to the work that is going to produce software. Story centered daily meetings help keep the discussion focused on how to efficiently move the stories toward completion and tend to reduce the amount of time spent on topics that are not going to help move stories from left to right.

 I have been in daily face-to-face meetings where 75% of the time is spent listening to each team member state that they are going to do their quarterly evaluation that day or that they did it yesterday. This is an extremely expensive use of time and it doesn't help move stories across the board toward completion.

You want to focus on the stories that are in-flight because those are the ones that are closest to providing value to the user. If the people working on the story tell the status and mention any impediments they are running into, they have covered all that is necessary. When someone mentions an impediment, other team members are probably going to try to jump in and help. This is exactly what should happen, but you cannot let each story turn into an hour-long troubleshooting session. If the team cannot solve the issue in 30 to 90 seconds, simply determine what the next step is going to be. Often the next step is for the people involved to discuss the issue right after the face-to-face meeting.

This is where most of the value of having a daily face-to-face meeting occurs. Everyone is in the same room and they discover things that need to be communicated. After the meeting, everyone can have those additional conversations while they are there face-to-face surrounded by the people who they may need to consult for clarifications or help. It should be very common for a stand-up meeting to end, a few people keep talking about a particular story, and then head down the hall to ask someone else in the organization a question that will help move that story forward.

Once you walk your way through the stories that are in-flight, it is often useful to check to see if there are any announcements that need to be made. This is a good place for team members to mention any general items that need to be communicated but are not story specific. For example, a developer might mention that they are going to be out for a doctor's appointment that afternoon so if anyone needs to discuss something they should do it before lunch. The team lead might mention that the version control system is going to be down for an upgrade in the morning, etc.

Usually, face-to-face meetings go better if someone is responsible for running them. This can be the team lead or manager, but it is a **team** meeting and you will usually get better ownership and buy-in if you let the team members take turns leading. Some teams work through who leads in a specific order—maybe alphabetically. You can let people just volunteer to lead each day, but then you are likely to get the same people every day. You also do not want a process that delays the start of your meeting by a few minutes each day while you figure out who runs it.

 Some teams create a chat bot to randomly select a member and post their name to the team messaging system five minutes before the daily meeting. This reminds everyone to get ready and helps prevents a discussion about who is going to run the meeting from taking up valuable time.

Talk to Users

- Business people and developers must work together daily throughout the project.
- The most efficient and effective method of conveying information to and within a development team is face-to-face conversation.

People who do not create software for a living typically assume that developers talk to users about what the users need, write some code to do what the user asked for, show it to the user to get feedback, and so on. They picture users and developers gathered around a table for discussions and around a computer screen to see the code in action. These are reasonable assumptions. It is obvious that developers and users are going to have to collaborate to create useful software. Unfortunately, that is not the way many organizations develop software applications. In fact, it almost seems like some places intentionally go out of their way to create processes that make it hard for users and developers to work together.

I was doing some consulting for a large bank that was trying to improve the efficiency of their software development process. After attending a few meetings, I realized that the person I thought was the user was not actually someone who was going to use the software. It turned out this person thought their job was specifically to keep the developers and users from talking to each other. I started asking what had prompted the creation of a role like that and traced it through the organization until someone finally told me that a famous big consulting company had told the bank to hire someone with that role as part of a set of recommendations several years earlier.

This still did not make much sense. After several months I happened to run into someone at a restaurant in New York who worked for the consulting company and discovered he had been a part of the project. I explained that the bank had introduced a new role tasked with keeping users and developers from talking to each other based on his company's recommendation. A horrified look crossed his face and he said, "No, that isn't at all what we recommended!"

Why does Agile make such a big deal of getting developers and users to talk to each other? Organizations have a tendency to create structures that keep this communication from taking place. Sometimes this is driven by political forces as people attempt to consolidate power by controlling the flow of information. Sometimes it is caused by efforts to make communication more efficient without fully understanding that the efficient creation of software requires two-way communication. Whatever the reason, companies find it very easy to create barriers to communication between developers and users. The bank in my story somehow was able to create new positions and hire people to fill those positions without anyone stopping to ask if creating a barrier to user/developer communications was really a good idea.

Software is created because it provides some type of value to someone. Those people are the users. The more layers an organization puts between the people who are creating the software and the people who are using it, the more inefficient the process is going to be. This does not mean your users need to be involved in every single detailed technical discussion about how code is being written, but it does mean they need to be close enough to the process to provide feedback that can guide the development so the end product will best meet their needs.

Regular Demos

- Our highest priority is to satisfy the customer through early and continuous delivery of valuable software.
- Build projects around motivated individuals. Give them the environment and support they need, and trust them to get the job done.
- Working software is the primary measure of progress.

Agile projects are built on trust, and the best way to establish trust is through transparency. Regular demos for users are one of the best ways for teams to be transparent about what progress has been made. Development should not be a black box from the user's perspective. The end users should be able to watch the software developing and provide feedback as it takes shape. Regular demos can help accomplish this.

Most users who have experienced a few software development projects are very familiar with projects that are scheduled to take 12 months that spend the first 10 months getting to 90% completion—and another 12 months finishing the remaining 10%. Demos help solve this problem in several different ways. First, demos help focus the development work on pieces of functionality that are actually usable. This may mean building some parts of the application in a simpler way, just so other parts can be demoed. This might seem trivial, but a focus on getting the application to a point where a feature is actually usable makes a huge difference in avoiding the false progress many projects see at the beginning that is followed by a dramatic slowdown at the end.

Second, the focus on creating functionality that can be demonstrated means that if the business owners are not happy with the timeline for when software is going to be ready to use, they can cut scope to finish sooner. If a team has not been focusing on software that can be demonstrated, the code that has been written is going to be much further from being in a usable state. Even if all the remaining scope is cut, there is still going to be a massive amount of work to get the "completed" features usable.

Third, demos help reduce the amount of rework that occurs. The simple fact is that no matter how hard users and developers try to communicate, there will be times where things will not be clear until they sit down and use the software. The sooner this happens, the less code will be built on incorrect assumptions.

I was working with a team that was building some software for the Treasury that was doing demos every two weeks. At one of the demos, the team walked through how to use the application for a particular function. The business owner questioned whether it was following the business rules correctly. Several of the users said it was correct, but after some more discussion, it became apparent that there were nuances to the business rules that even the users did not fully understand. Had it not been for the demo, this would not have been discovered until much later on and much more of the application would have been built on top of the faulty understanding.

 It is ideal to have an actual user or a business owner controlling the software in a demo. What if they do something that wasn't expected and it breaks? That is exactly why they **should** be doing it instead of a developer.

Demos need to demonstrate real working software. Walking through a series of screen mockups may be useful, but it does not count as a demonstration of working software. Demos should prioritize transparency over polish. If you have to manually load something into a database table to illustrate part of the user interface, do not hide that part from your demo. Everyone needs to know what has been built and what has not.

Demo Frequency

How often should you do software demos? It depends, but most projects have some sort of cadence that creates a natural place to demonstrate the functionality that has been built. If you are using sprints, it probably makes sense to do a demo at the end of each sprint. If you are not using sprints, you may need to pick something of an arbitrary length of time. For most projects, two weeks is usually a reasonable interval. For some projects, one week will work better. Some projects even work well with a demo every morning—especially if the developers are working from the other side of the world and demonstrate what they have completed at the end of their workday to stakeholders who are just starting theirs.

If demos are too frequent, it may be difficult to get high-level stakeholders to attend every one. On the other hand, with less frequent demos, if someone misses a single meeting they will not be able to participate in another demo for quite some time. Usually, longer periods between demos is more risky than the risk of some people occasionally not attending. Keep in mind, demos are establishing trust through transparency. For some high-level stakeholders, the knowledge that you are doing a demo that they *could* attend may provide a level of trust even if they are not able to actually be there.

There is a tendency to schedule demos around how much work is ready to demonstrate. While no one wants to have a meeting to demonstrate software and not have anything to show, it is important to carefully distinguish between a problem with demos being too frequent and a problem with not building in small enough slices of work. We explore this in more depth in the chapters on Better Stories and Deliver Small Changes. Not having anything to demonstrate is likely a symptom of the real problem. If a team does not have anything to demonstrate every two weeks, you should first try to redefine the work into smaller pieces so you will have new functionality in a state that you can demonstrate.

Do not forget you are striving for transparency over polish. If you need to demonstrate how the application lets you fill out a form but do not have the page that displays the data, show that the data gets saved into the database. It shows what work has actually been accomplished and maintains the transparency that is vital for high-trust teamwork to occur.

How To Run A Demo

If the idea of a "software demo" makes your organization think of a slick presentation with one person standing on a stage in front of a huge screen walking through a new piece of software, then call the demos something else. Your demos are not to put on a show or make the software look better or more complete than it is. The goal is to honestly communicate what features are complete and how they work.

If possible, you want the person driving the computer to be the person who will use the feature being demoed. This helps make sure that the demo shows what a real user is going to do. It also helps make sure that the demo does not look like a staged walkthrough of a mock-up.

Retrospectives

- At regular intervals, the team reflects on how to become more effective, then tunes and adjusts its behavior accordingly.
- The most efficient and effective method of conveying information to and within a development team is face-to-face conversation.

Change is expected and vital to progress. This applies to the code you are writing as well as your processes. Requirements may change to respond to the market or a new understanding of the problem being solved. It also applies to the way the team works together. Just because you did something one way yesterday, does not mean it is the way you should do it tomorrow. Agile explicitly says that teams need to take time to talk about how things are going and how they can work together better in the future.

Many teams do this through something called a retrospective. This is simply some time set aside to look for ways to work better. There are different ways to do retrospectives and you can find entire books specifically dedicated to opinions on the best process. In addition, there are many publications and articles on how to create continuous improvement in an organization. You will never exhaust all the possible ways to do retrospectives, but it is NOT important for them to be "perfect." Teams need to create a culture of gathering feedback and using it to create improvement. As long as you are taking steps toward that type of environment, you are doing it right.

To get the most value out of this type of team reflection, people need to be engaged. Simply having a meeting that you call a retrospective does not automatically guarantee that everyone is engaged in reflecting and making adjustments. A mature Agile team that has truly internalized the goal of reflecting on their processes to make improvements can easily have a retrospective process that looks entirely chaotic. I have observed some teams that have no formally scheduled retrospective because they do not need a schedule. Whenever a team member has a concern or an idea, they all simply take the time to talk about it, make a decision, and move forward.

One team I coached had a growing concern because they had not scheduled a retrospective in the last few months. While this was technically true, they had ad hoc retrospectives all the time—sometimes multiple times per week depending on what was going on and what needed to be addressed. Someone would send an instant message saying, "I don't think X is working very well, can we talk about it after stand-up?" After stand-up, they would discuss ways to improve, make a decision and then move forward. They still did formal retrospectives from time to time, but those were not where the bulk of the retrospective work was occurring.

I almost did not tell the story of this team because it is so easy to look at what is working for another team and simply mimic it in your own. This team had found a way to follow the Agile principle of regular reflection that worked well for their team dynamics, their individuals, their personalities, their working hours, etc. Your team will have its own dynamics, individuals, personalities, and working hours. Don't expect the optimal process for your team to look like the optimal process for another team.

A Simple Retrospective

Here is a simple way to do a retrospective. Place three sticky notes spaced out a few feet from each other on the wall. One should have a smiley face, the second a frowny face, and the third a thumbs up. Give everyone on the team their own sticky notes and ask them to write down things that they feel are going really well and put them under the smiley face, things that they think need improvement under the frown, and anything they want to call out positive about another team member under the thumbs up.

It can be good to limit everyone to only adding two notes under the frown to make sure people stay focused on their highest priority and to reduce the amount you have to sort through. You also want to make sure the team is not overly focused on negative aspects of how things are going. Looking for ways to improve can also mean celebrating your success and trying to keep doing things that are working well. No limit is usually needed for the smiley face and thumbs up. Set a time limit of 10 to 15 minutes for people to fill out their sticky notes and put them on the wall.

Have someone read through the smiley face and thumbs up notes. Usually, this does not take too long even if there are a large number of them. Since the frown section represents things you want to improve, you have to approach those more carefully. Read through them and try to group notes that represent the same thing by sticking them together. You may need to ask for clarification especially to see if the team agrees two notes represent the same core issue. The grouping helps make sure you do not end up splitting the vote count when the team selects what they want to work on.

 It is important that the team stay generally focused on things they can influence. If no one likes the president of your organization, there may not be any legal steps you can take to change that. You are looking for things you can solve or improve not just things to complain about.

Once the grouping is done, let everyone vote on what they would like to address. A simple approach is to letting everyone vote with a check mark, star, dot, or sticker on the issue they would most like to see addressed. Give everyone a limited number of votes—typically two is a good number.

When everyone is done voting, arrange the grouped notes in order with the highest votes at the top.

The next step is to pick some actionable step you can take to improve what the team has indicated as the most critical issue. You can try to address more than one if you have extra time, but it is probably best to start with one because you do not know how much discussion is going to be necessary.

The team is not trying to solve every aspect of the issue. They are trying to find something that they think will make things better and commit to doing that thing. I have seen some teams identify that broken builds were the most significant issue and then commit to making doubly sure that they run all the tests locally before checking back in code. Another team decided that their biggest issue was the way the rest of the organization perceived trivial problems with the software and committed to write a short article about their successes in the organization's monthly newsletter. Another team brought up issues in the way they worked together and made some commitments to practice more respect in their interactions.

Sometimes the issue can be fixed on the spot, but often you'll only be able to make a small commitment to something that makes an ongoing improvement. You may need to keep that commitment in front of the team. This can be done by posting it on the wall or spending 10 seconds to review it as part of the daily face-to-face meeting.

Retrospective Pitfalls

In a healthy team, everyone should be able to conduct the retrospective. Not all teams are healthy, however, and the person facilitating the retrospective could end up as the brunt of an emotional outburst. It can make sense to have someone who is comfortable with those dynamics and is skilled in keeping a pulse on how everyone is interacting lead the first few retrospectives.

I have participated in a few retrospectives that were, let us just say, "uncomfortable." Retrospectives tend to magnify any existing dysfunctions in the team. I have literally witnessed team members start jumping around screaming at each other until one of them stormed out of the room. Fortunately, that is not a normal retrospective, but it is a good reminder that the process of reflecting on ways to improve the way you work requires significant trust.

In the ideal world, every team member should be comfortable fully participating in the retrospective and even running the retrospective. As we mentioned above, some teams have worked together for years and have a high degree of trust where everyone feels empowered to call an ad-hoc retrospective whenever they see something that could be improved. Not everyone may be comfortable doing that–especially with a newly formed team. Sometimes it is helpful to have a facilitator run a few retrospectives and really focus on building trust until everyone is comfortable sharing their opinion and ideas. Ultimately though, the process of reflecting needs to be owned by and driven by the team itself.

The exact details of how you regularly reflect on ways to become more effective are not important. What is important is making sure that you are regularly investing time into looking for ways to improve, and that your whole team is comfortable speaking up about problems and potential solutions.

Better Stories

- Working software is the primary measure of progress.
- Our highest priority is to satisfy the customer through early and continuous delivery of valuable software.
- Simplicity–the art of maximizing the amount of work not done–is essential.

We have briefly touched on the topic of creating stories from the user perspective. In this chapter, we will consider how to create good stories in more detail.

The Importance Of Good Stories

In the Visualize Your Work chapter, we covered the importance of representing work visually because it is easy to see what has been done, what is being done, and what is yet to be done. We visualize our work through simple stories that describe what the user's world must look like in order to mark a story as complete. Here are some example stories using a typical story template.

As a registered user
I want to change my password
So I can keep my account secure

As a website visitor
I want to subscribe to the mailing list
So I can get product updates through email

As an admin user
I want to disable a user
So I can prevent unauthorized logins by past employees

As a mobile app user
I want to save all my data to the cloud
So I can access it from another device

There is not anything magical about this story template. If you find a better format for your team, by all means, use it. Having a template to follow is a good way to make sure no one suffers from writer's block when it is time to write down a story.

Our development efforts are driven by stories that represent our understanding of user needs. Stories written in ways that support our principles will foster good development practices. Stories written in ways that violate our principles will hinder good development practices. Anything we can do to increase the quality of our stories will make the rest of our development process more efficient.

The User Perspective

Effective stories start off as fiction. The setting is the world in which the user interacts with the software. Stories are written from the user's point of view and talk about things from the perspective of the user. The user perspective is critical because our principles say that we are going to define our progress based on giving the user the ability to do something with the software that they were not able to do before. If we are working on stories that are not creating business value for the customer, we are working on stuff that we have explicitly said is not going to count as progress.

So, how do we handle all the work we need to do that the user cannot see? How do we handle stories about the developer's world? How do we handle stories like this?

As a developer
I want to create a database that models the data
So I can store information the application needs

This is a bad story because it violates our principles for software development. Notice I said the story is bad, not the idea of having a database to store data. We definitely need a database to do this, but if we create this story, almost all of the application depends on it to be done first. We can complete this story and have no functionality to show our users—nothing they can actually use as working software. This violates our principles. Further, the information we need to acquire to complete this story will only be known when we figure out how we are going to build other parts of the system. So in effect, a story like this is both a prerequisite for and a dependency on every other story in the system.

When you have two things that both depend on the other

being done first, you have a recipe for deadlock. If you have ever worked on a story like this, you may have experienced a long period of time where the user is asking how things are going and the development team is saying, "Well, we have a bunch of setup work to do first before we can start working on the actual application."

There is another way. If you write your stories from the user perspective, you will build just the parts you need in order to create some value for the user. This likely will mean building some of the database, but only the pieces you need as you need them to complete each story.

Slices Of Value

If we want to create stories from the perspective of the user, we need to think about the application the way the user thinks about it. Developers tend to see the application as a stack. There is the hardware at the bottom. On top of that is the operating systems. Then comes the database and application server. Then we have a database access layer. Above that is the service or business logic layer. Somewhere above that is the code that is responsible for the user interface. Everything is stacked on top of each other like a cake. So, a developer is likely to think in terms of stories like:

As a developer
I want to create a service layer
So that the application logic is separated from the UI.

As a developer
I want to create a UI layer
So that the user can interact with the system.

Having a service layer is good. Having a user interface layer is good. Having stories to build each of these layers violates our principles, but it is easy to see why we might end up with stories like the above examples when we recognize the way developers think about an application. But what about the user? If our stories should be fiction from the user's point of view, we need to think about how they think about software applications.

A user will think of an application as a collection of behaviors they find valuable. They might think of an accounting system as consisting of the part that lets them create invoices, the part that lets them pay bills, and the part that lets them balance their accounts. They may know that creating an invoice means doing something in the GUI that gets passed on to the business rules and eventually ends up in the database, but that is not how the application is organized from their perspective.

If a developer sees an application as a collection of layers of cake that are stacked on top of each other, then users see the application as a collection of slices of cake that represent the different things they need to do. The fact that there is a database doing something toward the bottom of their slice of functionality is important, but only to the extent that it is necessary to support that slice of functionality.

If we could build software the same way users think about (and use) software, we could deliver value much more quickly. It is a beautiful thought, but everyone knows you cannot build a house by fully completing one room at a time. You cannot just slice the building project up like that. For that matter, you can't just create one slice of a multi-layer cake. You must start at the bottom, right? Absolutely–if you are building a house or a cake, but we are developing software. Code is not at all constrained by the same physical properties of buildings and desserts.

We actually can build a slice of functionality in software. If it seems hard to do, it is because we are too set in our ways of thinking of writing code as a construction or baking project where you have to complete one layer before putting anything above it. If you want to think of writing code in terms of some other activity, think of writing music. Bach did not have to write the entire lead voice in a fugue before he could go back and put the other voices in layer by layer. Instead, he could write a few bars for all the parts and try it out before moving on. Or, think of a symphony. Composers do not write hundreds of bars of bass drum before going back to add the next instrument. Instead, they write music several bars at a time. They may even finish a section and have it played to decide if they should continue, rework that part to make it better, or rethink their life choices. They work on creating valuable slices the same way that users think of our applications—-the same way we should develop our code.

 Just because you **cannot** do something when building a skyscraper does not mean it is impossible in code. Just because you **can** do something when writing a fugue does not mean you can do it when baking a cake. Analogies can be a great thinking tool, but make sure they are not limiting what you think is possible.

Splitting Stories

The size of a story can vary from team to team, but a reasonable starting place is creating stories that represent a few days worth of work. This may sound like a contradiction. We just discussed creating stories that represent an entire slice of user functionality, and now we are saying the slices should not take more than a few days. How can you create something useful for a user in a few days when you do not even have your database layer setup?

This is where the skill of splitting user stories becomes valuable. Yes, it is hard at first, but it is possible. If you can take a story that is going to require more than a few days and split it into several stories that are shorter, then you have done two things. First, you've created smaller units of work, so you can keep everything close to the same size. Second, you have now created the chance to prioritize the stories differently. This is a very valuable approach for the user because, if some of the resulting stories are lower priority and can be deferred until later, the user can instead focus on stories that are of higher value. Splitting stories is a way to increase the user return on investment.

How do you split stories? If we look back at our music example, we can find some ideas. Many composers of large-scale works would write the most important parts of their ideas in slices (measures) at a time for a reduced number of instruments, and then come back and fill in the supporting parts once they had proven out the overall idea. They would write the 20 percent that gave 80 percent of the value and then come back later and enhance it.

There are some pieces of functionality without which no value has been created. There are others that are very important, but their absence does not block value. Think about a checkout process for a web store. You add items to a cart, click the checkout button, log in so you do not have to type in your address, choose how you want to pay, type your payment information, and finally complete the purchase. Is there anything in that process that could be left out in providing the first slice of value? What if we did not bother with the login? Everyone can just type in their information to check out. We could also only implement one type of payment. It might even be possible to do away with the idea of a cart and just have a buy button that takes you to the payment page to purchase one item at a time.

So, what started out as a sizable story is now a matter of putting a single button on each product page that leads to a second page that lets you checkout. Perhaps you do not want to deploy it into production until it supports some additional features, but a user can try it out and definitely see that there is more value there than before. People can actually buy products, which is a pretty valuable thing to add, even if there are lots of enhancements coming later.

Now, you might look at this and say it is way too small. You can add a button and a single page in 45 minutes. Remember, we are building the full slice of functionality. That means you'll need to set up your data layer to handle recording the transaction. You may also need to get a certificate and turn on SSL to get the credit card processing to work. Many things need to be built to make this seemingly small story work. Of course, that is the point. You have to make the story small because you are going to have to touch a bunch of other layers to get it to work.

 It is extremely unlikely you will make your stories too small early in a project when using a story template as shown above.

With the rudimentary capability to buy a product, users can figure out what is the next most important piece of functionality they want to be able to exercise. Maybe it is the ability to buy more than one product at a time.

Perhaps they would rather see some part of the backend that displays the order so it can be shipped. By splitting the story to something smaller, they now have options on what to do next that they would not have if everything was all in the same big story.

Automation

- Working software is the primary measure of progress.
- Build projects around motivated individuals. Give them the environment and support they need, and trust them to get the job done.
- Continuous attention to technical excellence and good design enhances agility.
- Simplicity–the art of maximizing the amount of work not done–is essential.

A micromanaged team that does not have the right tools and is being measured by something like hours worked or lines of code written, will probably not have a lot of incentive to automate their work. However, we want a team that is dedicated to technical excellence, trusted to get the job done, trying to make things as simple as possible, and only counts working software as the measure of progress. Such a team will automate everything possible to make the process more efficient.

Any process that is error-prone, time-consuming, easy to forget, or generally disliked is a good candidate for automation. You want to avoid spending 100 hours automating something that will save you 5 minutes a year, but most software projects have no shortage of tasks and processes where automation yields significant efficiency gains.

The following is not meant to be an exhaustive list of everything that can be automated, but it should give you some general ideas.

Build Automation

Developers should be building their code many times an hour, so this is a great place to apply some automation. At the very least, it should be possible to build and test your code by executing a single command on the command line. Developers should be able to type a single line and build and test the entire application. Depending on the complexity of your application, this can be trivial or relatively complicated to implement. If you have tests that require a database, the ideal approach is for the build to handle setting up some type of database to test against. If you have a web user interface that tests run against, your build should stand up a web server and whatever other resources are necessary to execute the testing.

Fortunately, most build tools are designed to handle these types of situations, but it can take some time to get them working just right. However, the benefits of a single line build will continue throughout the life of the project.

With a single line build in place, it becomes significantly easier to add other automation like continuous integration and configure it to trigger a build and testing on every code update in version control. The goal of this type of automation is to make sure a developer gets notified if they accidentally check in a change that will break the build for others. Continuous integration can also check for compliance with security standards or other requirements.

This type of automation is crucial because the faster a team discovers a problem after it occurs, the easier it is to fix. The more time that elapses, the harder it is to identify the cause, the longer it takes to fix, and the more people are impacted.

I described a single line build, but what about using an integrated development environment (IDE)? Why not a single click build from within the IDE? I have seen many situations where the single line build makes it much easier to troubleshoot whether a problem is with the build or with your development tools. If there is always the ability to go to the command line and fire off a build, it is easy to tell if a problem is with the code or something in the IDE. Also, if you have multiple people working on a software project, you are going to need a way to integrate everyone's changes, run the build, and test them. Typically you want this to be done on a separate machine that is watching for new code and then kicking off a build whenever a developer submits a change. This is called a continuous integration server, and most of the systems that manage builds like this are not going to fire up an IDE and click on the build button. They are going to use the same mechanism you use for a single line build from the command line.

Deployment Automation

Many projects invest significant time manually going through the process of deploying software to servers in various environments. If you are simply going to deploy the software once, then maybe spending a few hours deploying it is not a bad use of time. However, if you want to be able to deploy small changes frequently, if your principles say that you are going to prefer deploying on shorter time frames, then the cost of deployment can easily become the bottleneck in getting new functionality to the user.

There are many tools for deploying code to servers. It can be as simple as a deployment script that gets executed by your continuous integration server or as complicated as a full DevOps ecosystem. The point is that you need to recognize that to be Agile you must have the ability to deploy frequently, and requiring a large investment of manual effort for each deployment will make that impossible.

Continuous delivery is a workflow that keeps your code in a ready-to-release state. At any time you can deploy the current release to production. Typically, this means setting up all the automation to build the code, test the code, create the deployment artifacts, and deploy them to a pre-production environment. With continuous delivery, automation takes any change to the code and "delivers" so it can be deployed to production. The actual deployment to production may be a matter of pushing a button or running a command.

Continuous deployment is the next logical step after continuous delivery. Changes are not only delivered **ready** for production–they are **deployed** to production. When you have a well designed automated process for lower environments, there is usually little technical difference between continuous delivery and continuous deployment. It is just a matter of repeating what was done in the pre-production environments. However, there are often significant governance issues involved in deploying to production, so the big barriers are often political.

> I coached a project for the US Treasury where there was a requirement that all deployments to production be done by someone in the change management department. This prevented full continuous deployment automation. Still, we were able to make the entire complex deployment process run with a single script. Running that script became the responsibility of the change management individual. It was not continuous deployment but achieved 99% of the benefit while still meeting governance requirements.

It is common to encounter resistance to the idea of automated deployments. Big organizations often have many people involved in the way software is deployed that may not be excited about using automation to do what they feel is their job. Maybe you are not able to get enough support to use automated deployments on production at first, but you can still establish a track record in your development and testing environments. Once you have something working and proven, it is easier to make a case for using the technology in production.

Tool Automation

Teams have all kinds of little unique things they need to do that can be automated. For example, I have seen teams build automation tools to replace the manual process of registering the IP address of team members who were working from home for the day. Other teams have created scripts to handle the way developers need to set up their environment, install organizational security certificates, bring up and down test environments, choose who is going to run the daily face-to-face meeting, or automate some convoluted change management processes for registering the use of a new software library.

To get the best use out of these little automation scripts and programs, they need to be checked into version control in a location where the whole team can use them. Not only does this let others benefit from the work, but it is easier to justify spending time building a small helpful tool when it is going to save time for the whole team.

Testing

- Working software is the primary measure of progress.
- Welcome changing requirements, even late in development. Agile processes harness change for the customer's competitive advantage.

There are many different ways to test software. It can be as simple as a developer running through what they think the user will do, or as complicated as an automated test suite that tries every button and text field while measuring what code gets executed and what does not.

The two principles above are very hard to follow without some type of automated testing. If working software is our primary measure of progress, we need some way of easily knowing if we have working software or if something is broken. Of course, you can do manual testing to prove the software works, but as the size of the application grows so does the time necessary for testing. If we want to make it easy to make changes even at the last minute, we need to have some way to quickly show that changes work as expected and not cause any unwanted side effects. This is hard to do if your test suite involves three weeks of effort by a team of testers. The only way to get a competitive advantage from making changes quickly is to have an automated way to verify those changes.

Having automated tests does not mean there is no human testing the application. You still need people to actually use the software and think about whether or not it will make sense to the end user. However, automated tests can let those people focus more on how the application works overall and less on mundane testing like trying every possible combination of filling out a form.

Automated Tests

Automated tests are tests that you can start and run without requiring your input. Ideally, these should be part of the build so they can be run by developers locally as well as on a continuous integration server. If your project is configured correctly, a developer should be able to launch a complete run of all the tests with a single click or single line command. The sooner developers can discover that something is broken, the easier it is to fix. The easier it is for them to run the tests, the more often they will run them.

A well-tested application may take a long time to run all the tests. It is common for well-tested projects to end up with enough tests that it takes several hours to run on a developer's laptop. This does not remove the need for having a one-step process to kick off the tests, Even at two hours, developers may sometimes need to run all the tests before committing their work. However, tests should be organized in ways that allow developers to test the part of the code they are working on locally before checking in and letting the full suite of tests run on the continuous integration server. A code base that is organized into logical modules makes this much easier to do. If organized well, a developer who makes a change to one module should be able to run the tests on that module and have fairly high confidence that they did not break something somewhere else before handing it over to the continuous integration server to verify this assumption.

Types Of Tests

There are three general types of tests. Each type concentrates on testing a different aspect of the software. Unit tests are focused on testing a small unit of code. Integration tests are focused on how the pieces come together and integrate with other services. Behavioral tests are focused on how the software behaves from the user's point of view. Notice that we say these tests are *focused* on these different things. In practice, there can be a good deal of overlap between the three types of tests.

Unit Tests

Unit tests are designed to exercise a tiny unit of software and verify it does what the developer expects. Unit testing might test that a particular method returns the proper values without trying to set up the entire application. A unit test typically does not need a database, web server, or other infrastructure in place in order to run. For example, a unit test for a function that transforms the output of a database shouldn't require setting up a database. The unit test should provide the value that would come from the database and then check the result. A unit test that verifies the ability of a method to create an email, should not actually require access to an email server to run.

There are many ways to "mock" the various pieces that these tests need, but if your application is designed well, you should be able to have unit tests for the various pieces of functionality with a minimal need for mocking out external services. In fact, one of the big advantages of test-driven development is the way that it tends to force you to write code that is modular and logically organized. Code that is not written in this way can be very difficult to test in small units that aren't dependent on other parts of the application.

Since unit tests are focused on testing very small units of code, they should run very quickly. Developers should be able to run the unit tests for the code they are working on in no more than a few seconds, and it is not uncommon for the unit testing run-time for hundreds of thousands of lines of code to be measured in seconds or a few minutes. The goal of unit tests is to give each developer the ability to quickly tell if a piece of code does what is expected and if it has any side effects on other code. Unit tests do not need to be something that users can understand because they deal with the internals of the software. Different types of tests deal with things from the user perspective.

Integration Tests

While unit tests focus on small units of functionality, integration tests cover how the pieces come together—how they integrate. Where unit tests might verify that a particular piece of code can transform data correctly without fetching it from the database, integrations tests would actually exercise that particular service with a database running and make sure that all the parts work together as expected. Where a unit test might test that a calculation is done correctly, an integration test might stand up a server and validate that the API accepts a request, does the calculation, and responds appropriately.

If you have designed your application with services that depend on each other, integration tests are going to test that these services all hook together and behave correctly. Obviously, these types of tests are going to run much slower than unit tests. Integration tests will probably make a little more sense to a user than the unit tests. A technical user will probably be able to see some of the business rules expressed in these types of tests. Still, integration tests focus mostly on things that are happening behind the scenes from the user experience.

Behavioral Tests

Behavioral tests look at the application from the user's per-spective. They should confirm that the application behaves as the user expects. Of the three types of tests, behavioral tests are typically the slowest to run because they come the closest to exercising the application the same way a user would.

For behavioral tests to be effective, they need to be written in a way that users can understand without becoming a programmer. This could be as simple as writing comments in the test code to tell the user what is happening, but there are a number of frameworks and tools like Cucumber that allow users and developers to specify what the application should do in natural language and then link it to code that exercises the application. This becomes an executable specification of the software.

For example, a Cucumber scenario might look like this:

Given I am on the demo page
When I convert the Arabic number 5
Then the roman numeral V is displayed

or

Given I am an unprivileged user
When I navigate to the settings page
Then a 403 error is shown

This format gives users and developers an excellent way to collaborate in discussing the features of the application.

The developer will then make this document executable by providing backing code which causes the natural language to execute against the application.

Not only do behavioral tests provide a way to test the application, the natural language aspect makes them an ideal reference of what users should expect the application to do in various circumstances. Unlike a document that gets out of date, the executable specification shows not only what the software is supposed to do, but what it is actually doing. If the software stops behaving the way that is specified, the tests will break and the build will fail.

Why Test?

As we have discussed, the **why** is very important to get value from any practice. Testing isn't an end in and of itself. Testing lets us show that the software is working. Since Agile says that working software is the way we define progress, testing allows a team to know if they are making progress or not. If you have worked on enough software projects, then you have doubtless seen projects that lacked tests where changes to one area broke existing functionality in another part of the application. I have actually seen projects that would spend a week developing code only to find that the software had less working functionality than it had at the beginning of the week. The new functionality may have worked, but so much was broken in the process that progress went backward in terms of working software.

As a teenager, I took a summer job with a roofing company. There was one very old roof in terrible shape where any effort to fix one leak would end up creating three more. The next time it rained, the new cracks were found and had to be fixed. However, the fix only created more leaks. They needed some way to make sure that fixing one problem did not make things worse. That is what tests do for software. They make sure that you can protect the progress you have achieved. Then future work moves you forward instead of backward.

This is especially true if you want to "welcome changing requirements." If you are trying to follow Agile, it means the customer is going to have a lot of flexibility in changing the target. There is simply no sane way to handle that type of fluctuation without being able to quickly tell if software is doing what it is supposed to be doing or not. If it takes six weeks to test your software manually and you really do not know how much progress you've made until the testing is done, then you are not leveraging change as a competitive advantage—no matter how quickly you can pivot on what is being developed. You simply cannot obtain feedback on your progress and use it for making useful decisions without a good automated testing strategy.

Deliver Small Changes

- Our highest priority is to satisfy the customer through early and continuous delivery of valuable software.
- Deliver working software frequently, from a couple of weeks to a couple of months, with a preference to the shorter timescale.
- Working software is the primary measure of progress.

To continuously deliver valuable software, we have to deal with smaller changes. Short timescale delivery of working software requires a way of delivering small units of functionality all the way into production on a regular basis.

We already talked about the need for small stories. Not only should your stories be small in size, but you also should be able to deliver a small number of stories at a time. This requires an automated approach to software delivery that can be difficult to justify for teams that only plan to deliver software a few times each year.

Risk In Development

Any time you make a change to software, there is a risk that the change will have unwanted side effects. Automated testing can dramatically reduce this risk, but it is always present. If you release two small changes, then there are two ways they can interact with each other. If you release four changes, you now have 12 possible interaction points. By the time you get to 12 changes, you have 132 possible interaction points.

Deploying two small changes to production is not as risky because there are so few things that can go wrong. With just a few changes, it is much easier to look at the code that is going to change and agree on what those changes will do. You can mentally reason about what is going to happen if you are moving a system from a known working state to a slightly different state where the changes are small enough you can easily understand them. Even if a bug slips through, the effort required to identify the problem when you are dealing with 20 lines of changed code is much less than when dealing with 5,000. Not only is it easier to figure out, but it is easier to fix. When you are trying to deploy a new version with a massive number of changes, you lose this luxury.

Deployment Frequency

We can say we want deployments with a small number of changes, but it is important to recognize the logical consequences. **Small** deployments almost always imply **frequent** deployments. If you want to deploy changes to fewer lines of code, you must increase the frequency of your deployments.

Let's say you are currently deploying code once each month that represent changes we can quantify as about 800 hours of development effort. If you want your deployments to represent something closer to 100 hours of development effort, you will need to change your deployments from once per month to twice each week. Otherwise, the team's ability to deliver functionality is going to vastly outpace your ability to deploy. The other option would be to discard 7/8ths of your development capability.

We can represent our risk on the development side with this graph. To make the risk go down, we have to increase the deployment frequency.

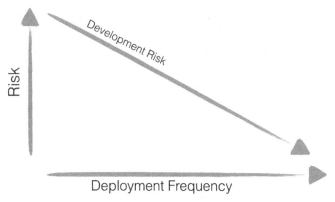

Development risk vs. deployment frequency

Most organizations see the value of making a small number of changes to the system and agree in principle that there is value in delivering software on shorter timescales. We have focused on the risk associated with big infrequent changes to the code, but there are significant business advantages as well. Where we start running into trouble is when we look at what else needs to change in order to fully support doing this–in particular, the way most organizations handle the deployment of software.

Risk In Deployment

While most companies recognize that deploying a large number of development changes increases the risk that something will go wrong, they usually justify their approach by pointing to the number of things that have gone wrong in the **deployment** process. If deployments have a high risk of breaking something, they reason that risk can be lowered by deploying less frequently. If there is a 50% chance that a mistake will occur in deployment, then doing two deployments creates a 75% probability of a mistake. This leads to the perception that frequent deployment necessarily increases risk.

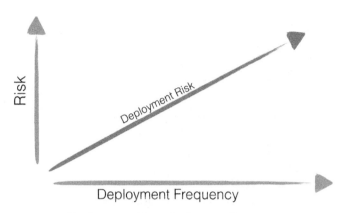

Deployment risk vs. deployment frequency

Organizations that see deployment risk in this way have the goal of balancing the **development risk** of new code doing something unexpected with the **deployment risk** that something will go wrong while putting the new version into production. Since the more frequently code is deployed, the smaller the number of changes in each deployment, you end up with a risk vs. deployment frequency that looks something like this graph. These organizations usually try to achieve a deployment frequency somewhere around the intersection of the two arrows. This is rational behavior if you assume that the risk profiles for development and deployment are both fixed and slanted in opposite directions.

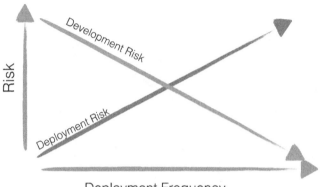

Deployment risk vs. development risk

There are two problems with this. First, it assumes that the deployment process is necessarily a high-risk event. Second, it overlooks the fact that doing deployments infrequently means the process is less well known and less exercised, so the infrequency actually increases risk.

Reducing Risk

Clearly, it would be better if both of the risk arrows sloped in the same direction. We can lower the risk of the development by more thorough testing, but it does not change the slope of that risk. It is still going to be less risky to release fewer changes at a time from the development point of view. However, deployment is a different story. If a team only deploys twice a year, the payback of automating the deployment is very low and the risk of a missed step or something not working correctly is very high. On the other hand, for a team that is deploying every day, the cost of doing things manually is simply too high to justify, and there is a significant return on any investment in automation. If we want to reduce the risk of deployment we must create a deployment process that is designed to be robust, failsafe, and efficient. This is done through automation and deployment testing.

DevOps is the movement representing practices that promote this approach. From an extremely pragmatic view, your deployment process needs two things. First, you need a way to automate the deployment process. Second, you need a way to test the deployments. Automation can be as complicated as a full implementation of DevOps tools or as simple as writing deployment scripts. The important part is to make sure it handles the entire deployment process. If you have scripts to deploy your code, but you still need a DBA to manually run updates to the database you have not really achieved automation.

From a testing standpoint, you should not be testing your deployment in production. The risk is simply too great for production to be the first place the deployment process is exercised. Staging environments that use the same deployment tools and processes lower the chance of something unexpected happening in production. We test our code to make sure there are no bugs. We need to do the same thing to the steps and procedures that deploy our code.

Aligning Development and Deployment Risk

If these two pieces are implemented properly, you can change the slope of the arrow of the deployment risk to match the slope of the development risk. This change in slope is possible because once you have automated and tested your deployments, there is less risk in exercising that mechanism often and more risk in only exercising it infrequently. If you are exercising your deployment scripts and processes every week and something does not work in one of your testing environments, you only have a small number of changes since it last worked correctly. On the other hand, if you have six months of changes, it will be exponentially more difficult to figure out what went wrong because of the large number of changes that have accumulated.

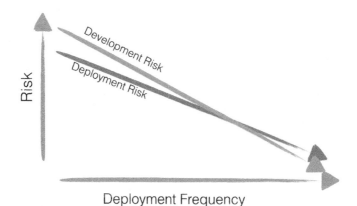

Deployment Frequency

Deployment risk and development risks aligned

Once you have the slopes headed the same direction, the conflict between development risk and deployment risk goes away, and you can now work toward lowering both types of risk by increasing the deployment frequency and lowering the number of changes deployed at the same time. With this in place, the team can work toward continuous delivery of valuable code, frequent delivery of working software, and counting working software as the primary measure of progress—all Agile principles we listed at the beginning of this chapter.

Understanding Business Value

- Welcome changing requirements, even late in development. Agile processes harness change for the customer's competitive advantage.
- Our highest priority is to satisfy the customer through early and continuous delivery of valuable software.

These two principles are interesting because they provide something of a litmus test development teams can use to determine if they are actually trying to be Agile.

Imagine the following scenario. Your team has been working very hard to get the first usable piece of a new feature completed and deployed to production. Your customer comes in one day and says, "So that thing we told you was really important? It turns out to not be as important as we thought, but we've got this new set of features that we want to start working on instead."

How does your team react?

A. "Why can't they get their act together and figure out what they want us to work on? They obviously don't have any idea what they are doing."

B. "That sounds great! Good thing we can just switch what we are working on because this change sounds like it will drive a lot more business value."

If your organization is really tuned for agility, if your developers are working closely with the business owners, if you have established a strong foundation of trust that can only come from good transparent communication, then your team should be able to react to the change in a positive way.

Most developers feel valuable because they can write code that works correctly. Far fewer see their value in providing a competitive advantage by changing what they are working on quickly. When developers *do* feel this way, it is a sign of a healthy Agile mentality and strong collaboration between the developers and business interests. Developers will not feel this way unless they understand the business value that is driving the code they are creating.

I routinely see teams of developers make big changes to the way that they are developing software. I have seen teams suggest rewriting significant portions of the code base to use a new framework or even rewriting the entire application in a new language. Sometimes I am amazed at how easy it is for a team to reach consensus to do significant rework in order to make technical improvements. Why is this?

Within a development team, there is communication. There is discussion. There are arguments. There is debate. Developers can reach agreement on the value of even deep technical changes because they are immersed in the details. They understand the tradeoffs, the costs, and the value of technical changes.

For a team to welcome changes, they must know enough about the cost and value of those changes to truly understand the business value of what they are doing.

> A story is told of two assembly line workers doing similar work in two different companies. When the first was asked what he was doing, he said he was screwing two pieces of metal together with a bolt and nut. The individual in the other company said, "I'm building cars!"

If developers are going to really embrace change, they must understand the drivers of change. They must understand how the code provides value in the big picture. It is easy for developers to understand the value and costs of change driven by technical considerations. To embrace change driven by business considerations, developers must understand the business value of the code they write.

This can be much more difficult than it initially sounds. A recent conversation I had with some developers concerning testing highlighted this difficulty. A few developers were talking about optimizing all tests for greatest speed. While I agreed to a point, I commented that the testing needs to be done with an understanding of how it provides business value because ultimately that is the goal. This was not very popular. At first, I was surprised my statement didn't have universal acceptance, but, if I put on my developer hat and think about "ideal" software development, I can easily prioritize "perfect" software engineering over the business value the software development process provides.

Change is hard. Do not expect it to be easy, but when everyone can clearly see how their efforts are creating business value, it lays a foundation to align technical skills with business needs in exceptionally valuable ways.

Sustainable Continual Improvement

- Agile processes promote sustainable development. The sponsors, developers, and users should be able to maintain a constant pace indefinitely.

As we close this short book, it is important to remember that Agile is not something you achieve and then move on. Agility is an ongoing process. The moment a team feels they have "arrived" and no longer have to work hard to respond to change is the moment where they stop being Agile. This is why I tend to be a bit suspicious of Agile "transformations." A "transformation" is something that is easy to sell because it has a start and an end. After that, the transformation is "complete." Successful Agile teams are those that have nurtured and honed their culture, environment, and attitudes to adapt to unknown future change. An Agile team is a team that is prepared to evolve quickly. If the result of a "transformation" is a team that has started this evolutionary process, then I can get behind that. However, if a team is simply transformed from one set of rigid rules to another not quite so rigid, it misses the point. That does not mean that transformed-but-not-evolving teams will not see any benefit, but it is not the same as a team that is truly prepared to adapt going forward.

This long-term ability to adapt is essential. Many of the Agile principles imply this type of thinking, but the principle shown above is much more explicit. It points toward the need for teams to be able to operate over long periods of time and continually adjust and improve.

So much software creation is exceptional, and I do not mean that in a good way. It is exceptional, not because it is above average in quality or some other metric, but because success is only realized by doing all kinds of things that are exceptions to the way everyone agrees we should be producing software. Teams are asked to work weekends for extended periods of time. Individuals are expected to work 70-hour weeks on a regular basis. Schedule slips result in cutting testing or other important quality functions. All of these things are exceptions to the way we know we should work, and it is not sustainable.

That is not to say that there will never be any exceptions in creating software—the whole point of Agile is responding to change—but many projects begin with plans that are clearly unsustainable. Agile processes help promote habits that are sustainable, but the gains need to be invested in creating better efficiency—not just going back to unsustainable practices, but starting at a higher threshold.

This book covered a number of practices that can be very useful ways to follow Agile values and Agile principles, but always remember that if you want to be Agile you have to focus on what works for your team. If your team just takes practices you see in other teams and tries to mimic the actions without understanding the principles, you are doing the same thing as the guy wearing coconut headphones trying to wave planes down from the sky.

You have probably heard the story about five chimpanzees placed in a cage with a banana at the top of a ladder. Whenever a chimp goes for the banana, all of the chimps get sprayed with cold water. Soon all the chimps ignore the banana. Then one of the chimpanzees is swapped out with another. This new chimp sees the banana and heads for it only to be attacked by the others who do not want to be sprayed with water again. The chimps are exchanged one by one until none of them have ever been sprayed by water, yet they have all learned not to go for the banana and to attack anyone who does.

As far as I can tell, no one ever conducted such an experiment. I do not work with chimpanzees, so I have no idea whether they would actually behave like this. I do work with humans, and we (myself included) do stuff like this all the time. I have had people get angry when I asked why the team was following a particular practice. I definitely remember being in situations where I felt like the mythical chimpanzee who got attacked. "Well, I guess I found out what happens if you bring **that** up!"

You must be willing to tweak and improve your practices when you find they can be adjusted to better follow Agile principles and the only way to do this is to make sure you are always asking why. If you are not doing this, you are not following the spirit behind Agile. When everyone knows why you are following a particular practice, it sets up an environment to change, adapt, and improve over time. It keeps everyone focused on the value that practice is providing and what principles it is supporting. Without this, it is easy to start to believe that the practice itself is the goal.

Whether you are just starting your Agile journey or looking to tune your existing efforts, always stay focused on the reason behind each action. That is the only way to continually improve your effectiveness as an Agile team.

Glossary

Rather than simply define words previously presented in the book, this glossary is an attempt to provide some general definitions of terms likely to be encountered by teams starting out with Agile. Many of these terms have nuances that cannot be fully explored here, but these definitions should provide a reasonable starting point.

For many, the real value of this list of terms may be less as a reference to find definitions and more as a starting point to find the names of new practices, tools, and approaches that merit further research to help solve the particular challenges your team is facing.

Acceptance Test Driven Development (ATDD)
> A practice where development is not started until there are clear descriptions of how the user would verify that a new feature is implemented correctly. The development work is then driven by these descriptions. The descriptions may or may not be automated. Behavior Driven Development is a specific way of doing Acceptance Test Driven Development.

Agile
> A set of principles and values codified in the Agile Manifesto by a group of 17 individuals who had come together to talk about alternatives to heavy

weight documentation driven software development approaches.

Backlog

A list of work to be done. When a team has capacity, items are selected from the backlog to be worked on. Prioritization of the backlog determines which features are developed next. This prioritization process should be driven by the business interests.

Behavior Driven Development (BDD)

The practice of driving development based on the desired behavior of the system usually from the standpoint of user action and expected result. This is done through an executable specification written so non-developers can understand the desired behavior of the system. By executing the specification, the application is shown to function in the desired way. This approach is useful in the process of defining requirements and in limiting the scope of development work to exactly what is needed.

Continuous Delivery

The practice of taking every change to a code base through a build, testing, and deployment process. The build is typically deployed to an environment that is similar enough to production to prove that the release and deployment will work in production.

Continuous Deployment

A practice that builds on continuous delivery by

automatically deploying each build to production once the code and deployment process has proven it works correctly.

Continuous Integration

The practice of regularly integrating the work from all developers and testing it. Usually this is done on a continuous integration server that is set to do a full build and execute automated tests each time a developer checks in a change to the code base.

Cycle Time

The amount of time between a cycle. This could be a repeating process like the delivery of a release to production. It could also be the time between two well-defined start and end points. For example, the point where work is requested and the point where work is completed. See lead time, velocity.

Definition of Done

The criteria the team has agreed upon to say that a particular user story is complete. Agreement on this definition avoids situations where work that is thought to be complete ends up requiring more effort before it can actually be used. Some teams will consider work to be done once it has been programmed, integrated with the rest of the code base, and fully tested. On other teams, features are not considered done until they are deployed to production and in use.

DevOps

The practice of taking useful approaches from development and applying them to operations. This includes the use of source control, automation, and testing. It also encourages the view that development and operation processes should be more collaborative with a focus on delivering customer value rapidly and safely.

Extreme Programming

Extreme programming is an Agile development framework. It grew out of an effort by a team at Chrysler to take practices that produce better software and see what would happen if they were done in extreme ways. For example, since automated tests help produce better software, the team took the extreme step of writing tests before the code was even written. This practice is called test driven development. Since code reviews were known to increase the quality of software, the team started conducting real-time code reviews with two people working together to write code. This practice is now known as pair programming.

Integration Test

A test that verifies that the integration of various functions works correctly together. Instead of testing a single method or function of code, integration tests verify that the pieces of an application work together. Often this means testing that code talking to a database or application server executes correctly and that all the different parts integrate together. See unit test.

Iteration

A cycle in software development that typically culminates in delivering features that are ready for the user. See sprint.

Iterative Development

A cyclical process where software is delivered in smaller units rather than all at once at the end of the project. This allows feedback from what has been built to be incorporated into the next cycle. Iterative development contrasts with waterfall development.

Kanban

A system to balance work capability with demand invented by Toyota to improve the efficiency of inventory and assembly work. It was inspired by the way that grocery stores were able to minimize waste of perishable goods while still meeting customer demand. Kanban literally means "sign" and was the name of the signal cards passed back and forth on the factory floor to request that parts be moved to where they were needed and reordered as necessary. Kanban provides a means of optimizing the flow of work through a system. It is particularly useful in making the overall system efficiency more transparent and avoiding situations where high utilization of individual parts of the system create inefficiencies in the whole.

Kanban Board

A visual representation of work in a Kanban system. This is especially useful in knowledge work where there aren't physical parts, supply bins and inventory stations where physical cards can be attached and removed. A typical Kanban board for software will show pieces of functionality moving from planning, to development, to a completed state, to deployment.

Kanban Method

Typically refers to a method built around applying a Kanban system to knowledge work. Kanban method is best seen as a process that uses Kanban systems to make continual evolutionary improvement with a focus on the continuous flow of work rather than iterations.

Lead Time

The time elapsed between the placing of an order and delivery of that order. In software, this typically measures the cycle time between a feature being requested and when it is delivered. There is some degree of variation in the precise start and end points used by different teams. For example, some teams start measuring when a feature is requested, while others start when work is begun. See cycle time and velocity.

Pair Programming

A practice from Extreme Programming where two developers work together to write code. Typically this involves two people physically working at one computer and discussing the code as it is written. Pair programming comes from the idea that code reviews are so valuable that there are situations where doing them in real-time is more efficient than having two people work separately and then doing code reviews after a feature is developed.

Persistent Chat

An approach to facilitate shared knowledge in distributed teams using an on going group chat with all team members. Rather than having chats between individuals, they are done in the chat where all members can read them. This attempts to somewhat reproduce the ability to overhear conversations in a teamroom that help disseminate information through a team.

Persistent Video Conference

An approach to creating the experience of a team room with distributed teams. Each team member participates in a video conference with the rest of the team during their working hours every day so everyone can hear and see each other. A persistent video conference may also be used to link multiple team rooms together with each other and with remote individuals.

Retrospective

> A common ceremony on Agile teams where they reflect on how well their practices are working and try to find ways to work more efficiently going forward. Often these are done at the end of a one or two-week iteration.

SCRUM

> SCRUM is a framework for team collaboration using an iterative process referred to as sprints. A sprint consists of a planning phase where work is selected, a work phase, a demo for stakeholders, and a retrospective. This process is repeated on a regular basis—typically every one or two weeks.

Stand-up Meeting

> A common ceremony on Agile teams where everyone meets face-to-face once each day for 15 minutes in a standup meeting with the goal of moving work forward in the process.

Story Points

> A way to compare relative time it will take to complete specific user stories. A story that has been assigned four story points should take about half as much time to complete as a story that is assigned eight story points. A number of other terms are used to represent this same idea. "Gummy bears" or "NUTs" (nebulous units of time) are two other terms that serve the same purpose.

Sprint

An iteration in SCRUM that typically lasts one or two weeks. A sprint is a single cycle in the iterative development process used by SCRUM.

Team Room

Space assigned for a team to work together in order to maximize face to face communication.

Test Driven Development (TDD)

A practice where production code is only written in response to a failing test. To create new functionality, a developer first writes a test that would pass if the functionality existed and runs it to verify that the test fails. The production code is written in order to make the test pass. The approach can benefit efficiency by focusing work on small incremental changes and in many cases helps produce code that is modular and easier to modify in the future.

Three Amigos

Refers to three points of view that need to be represented in the discussion of new features. The first point of view is that of the business. The business can speak to the value of a proposed feature, what it is supposed to do, and understand the impact of proposed trade-offs. The second is the development perspective. Developers understand the technical approach to creating a new feature. The third is the testing perspective which represents the need to prove a feature works as intended. Efficient balance between the cost and value of a particular feature is much easier to achieve when all three views are represented in the discussion of new work.

Unit Test

Code written as an automated test that proves a function or similar small unit of production code does what the developer expects. Unit tests typically run quickly and don't require infrastructure support, like databases and webservers, in order to run.

User Story

A simple way of representing development work by creating a short narrative about what a feature will look like from a particular user's point of view. User stories allow teams to easily talk about a feature at a level that is reasonably intuitive to understand but not so detailed that it impedes conversations.

Velocity

In physics velocity is the distance covered in a given period of time, for example, feet per second. In software development, velocity refers to the amount of development work completed in a period of time– usually an iteration. The amount of work is often measured in stories, story points, or features.

Version Control

The way teams manage the process of making changes to the code base. Version control tools allow multiple users to make changes to the code base at the same time and provide methods to merge those changes together while avoiding conflicts. Git and Subversion are two common version control tools.

Waterfall Development

An approach to software development where each stage of work is completed before moving on to the next. For example, the requirements are fully defined for the entire project before starting on the design, etc. Delivery of the software occurs all at once at the end of the project. Waterfall stands in contrast to iterative development.

54176797R00066

Made in the USA
Middletown, DE
13 July 2019